FOR LAUGHING OUT LOUD

FOR LAUGHING OUT LOUD

POEMS TO TICKLE YOUR FUNNYBONE

FOR LAUGHING OUT LOUD

POEMS TO TICKLE YOUR FUNNYBONE

Selected by JACK PRELUTSKY

Illustrated by MARJORIE PRICEMAN

RED FOX

To Tony, Elizabeth, and Blake

—*J.P.*

To Mom and Dad

—*M.P.*

A Red Fox Book.
Published by Random House Children's Books,
20 Vauxhall Bridge Road, London SW1V 2SA.

First published in the USA by Alfred A Knopf, Inc, New York 1991
First published in Great Britain by Hutchinson Children's Books 1992
Red Fox edition 1994

1 3 5 7 9 10 8 6 4 2

RANDOM HOUSE UK Limited Reg. No. 954009
ISBN 0 09 923731 8

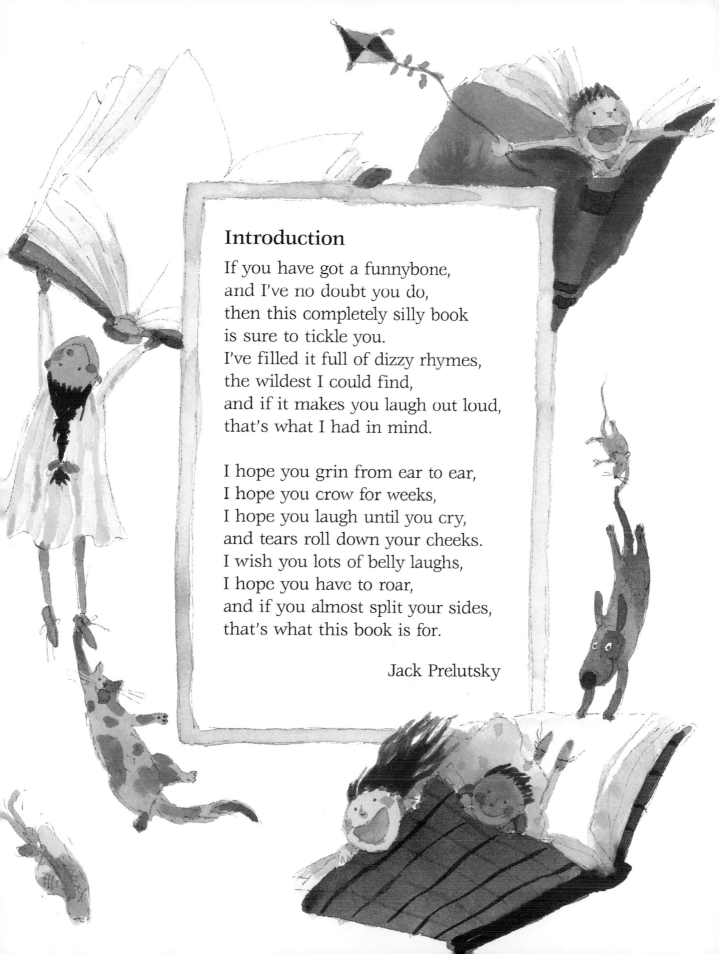

Introduction

If you have got a funnybone,
and I've no doubt you do,
then this completely silly book
is sure to tickle you.
I've filled it full of dizzy rhymes,
the wildest I could find,
and if it makes you laugh out loud,
that's what I had in mind.

I hope you grin from ear to ear,
I hope you crow for weeks,
I hope you laugh until you cry,
and tears roll down your cheeks.
I wish you lots of belly laughs,
I hope you have to roar,
and if you almost split your sides,
that's what this book is for.

Jack Prelutsky

Laughing Time

It was laughing time, and the tall Giraffe
Lifted his head, and began to laugh:

Ha! Ha! Ha! Ha!

And the Chimpanzee on the ginkgo tree
Swung merrily down with a *Tee Hee Hee:*

Hee! Hee! Hee! Hee!

"It's certainly not against the law!"
Croaked Justice Crow with a loud guffaw:

Haw! Haw! Haw! Haw!

The dancing Bear who could never say "No"
Waltzed up and down on the tip of his toc:

Ho! Ho! Ho! Ho!

The Donkey daintily took his paw,
And around they went: Hee-Haw! Hee-Haw!

Hee-Haw! Hee-Haw!

The Moon had to smile as it started to climb;
All over the world it was laughing time!

Ho! Ho! Ho! Ho! Hee-Haw! Hee-Haw!
Hee! Hee! Hee! Hee! Ha! Ha! Ha! Ha!

William Jay Smith

Nuts to You and Nuts to Me!

Nuts to you and nuts to me!
Walnut, chestnut, hickory,
Butter-, coco-, hazel-, pea-
Nuts to you and nuts to me!

Mary Ann Hoberman

Oodles of Noodles

I love noodles. Give me oodles.
Make a mound up to the sun.
Noodles are my favorite foodles.
I eat noodles by the ton.

Lucia and James L. Hymes, Jr.

4

Forty Performing Bananas

We're forty performing bananas,
in bright yellow slippery skins,
our features are rather appealing,
though we've neither shoulders nor chins,
we cha-cha, fandango, and tango,
we kick and we skip and we hop,
while half of us belt out a ballad,
the rest of us spin like a top.

We're forty performing bananas,
we mambo, we samba, we waltz,
we dangle and swing from the ceiling,
then turn very slick somersaults,
people drive here in bunches to see us,
our splits earn us worldly renown,
we're forty performing bananas,
come see us when you are in town.

Jack Prelutsky

Banananananananana

I thought I'd win the spelling bee
   And get right to the top,
But I started to spell "banana,"
   And I didn't know when to stop.

William Cole

5

The Optimist

The optimist fell ten stories,
    And at each window bar
He shouted to the folks inside:
    "Doing all right so far!"

Anonymous

Somebody Said
that It Couldn't Be Done

Somebody said that it couldn't be done—
But he, with a grin, replied
He'd never be one to say it couldn't be done—
Leastways, not 'til he'd tried.
So he buckled right in, with a trace of a grin;
By golly, he went right to it.
He tackled The Thing That Couldn't Be Done!
And he couldn't do it.

Anonymous

The Sad Story of a Little Boy That Cried

Once a little boy, Jack, was oh! ever so good,
Till he took a strange notion to cry all he could.

So he cried all the day, and he cried all the night,
He cried in the morning and in the twilight;

He cried till his voice was as hoarse as a crow,
And his mouth grew so large it looked like a great O.
It grew at the bottom, and grew at the top;
It grew till they thought that it never would stop.

Each day his great mouth grew taller and taller,
And his dear little self grew smaller and smaller.

At last, that same mouth grew so big that—alack!—
It was only a mouth with a border of Jack.

Anonymous

Boo Hoo

Mabel cried as she stood by the window,
Mabel cried as she stood by the door.
Mabel cried and her tears filled three buckets;
Mabel cried as she sat on the floor.

Mabel cried for oh so many hours,
Mabel cried for oh so many more.
With her tears then she watered her flowers;
With the rest then she mopped up the floor.

Arnold Spilka

7

Norman Norton's Nostrils

Oh, Norman Norton's nostrils
Are powerful and strong;
Hold on to your belongings
If he should come along.

And do not ever let him
Inhale with all his might,
Or else your pens and pencils
Will disappear from sight.

Right up his nose they'll vanish;
Your future will be black.
Unless he gets the sneezes,
You'll *never* get them back!

Colin West

Be Glad Your Nose Is on Your Face

Be glad your nose is on your face,
not pasted on some other place,
for if it were where it is not,
you might dislike your nose a lot.

Imagine if your precious nose
were sandwiched in between your toes,
that clearly would not be a treat,
for you'd be forced to smell your feet.

Your nose would be a source of dread
were it attached atop your head,
it soon would drive you to despair,
forever tickled by your hair.

Within your ear, your nose would be
an absolute catastrophe,
for when you were obliged to sneeze,
your brain would rattle from the breeze.

Your nose, instead, through thick and thin,
remains between your eyes and chin,
not pasted on some other place—
be glad your nose is on your face!

Jack Prelutsky

An Old Man from Peru

There was an old man from Peru
Who dreamed he was eating his shoe.
    He awoke in the night
    And turned on the light
And found it was perfectly true.

Anonymous

Neet People

The people of Neet have triangular feet
With a toe on each point, six in all;
They stand up like brooms
In the corners of rooms,
In foyers, and closets, and halls.

The people of Neet are quite fond of their feet
Which look something like pieces of pie;
And they're happy to stay
In the corners that way
For the people of Neet are all shy.

The corners in Neet are all filled up with feet
For they stand there from morning till night;
The people of Neet
Are all gentle and sweet
But they aren't especially bright.

Lois Simmie

At the Beach

—Johnny, Johnny, let go of that crab!
 You have only ten fingers, you know:
 If you hold it that way, it is certain to grab
 At least one or two of them. Please, let go!

—Thank you, Daddy, for teaching not scolding,
 But there's one thing I think you should know:
 I believe it's the crab that is doing the holding—
 I let go—OUCH!—ten minutes ago!

John Ciardi

The Flying Fish

"Oh, why can't I sing?" sighed the Flying Fish,
 "On music I simply dote.
I'm half a bird, and it seems absurd
 That I haven't a single note."

But the Dolphin said, "I'll forgive your want.
 You will make a delightful dish:
Music is good, but I prefer food,"—
 And he swallowed the Flying Fish.

J. J. Bell

About the Teeth of Sharks

The thing about a shark is—teeth,
One row above, one row beneath.

Now take a close look. Do you find
It has another row behind?

Still closer—here, I'll hold your hat:
Has it a third row behind that?

Now look in and . . . Look out! Oh my,
I'll *never* know now! Well, good-bye.

John Ciardi

The Water's Deep

The water's deep,
The sharks are thin,
The current's strong
So COME ON IN!

Colin McNaughton

How to Tell a Tiger

People who know tigers
　Very very well
All agree that tigers
　Are not hard to tell.

The way to tell a tiger is
　With lots of room to spare.
Don't try telling them up close
　Or we may not find you there.

John Ciardi

The Tiger

The Tiger is a perfect saint
As long as you respect him;
But if he happens to say *ain't*,
You'd better not correct him.

John Gardner

Samantha

In the jungle skipped Samantha,
For her troubles to forget,
When she met a hungry panther
Who'd not had his breakfast yet.

But Samantha had some flowers,
So she gave the beast the bunch.
They became good friends for hours—
Then he ate her up for lunch.

Colin West

The Walrus

The Walrus lives on icy floes
And unsuspecting Eskimoes.

Don't bring your wife to Arctic Tundra
A Walrus may bob up from undra.

Michael Flanders

Ruthless Rhyme

Poor Grandma's hair hung all awry,
  So we washed it during days of heat,
Then hung her upside-down to dry
  On the clothes-line by her stockinged feet.

J. A. Lindon

Higgledy-Piggledy
Keeps His Room Tidy

Higgledy-Piggledy
  keeps his room tidy.
He fluffs up his pillows
  and smooths down his spread.
He straightens out drawers
  and he dusts every corner.

(Just wait till I dump
all my trash on his bed!)

Myra Cohn Livingston

A Young Lady of Crete

There was a young lady of Crete,
Who was so exceedingly neat,
  When she got out of bed
  She stood on her head,
To make sure of not soiling her feet.

Anonymous

Garbage Delight

Now, I'm not the one
To say No to a bun,
And I always can manage some jelly;
If somebody gurgles,
"Please eat my hamburgles,"
I try to make room in my belly.
I seem, if they scream,
Not to gag on ice cream,
And with fudge I can choke down my fright;
But none is enticing
Or even worth slicing,
Compared with Garbage Delight.

  With a nip and a nibble
  A drip and a dribble
  A dollop, a walloping bite:
  If you want to see grins
  All the way to my shins,
  Then give me some Garbage Delight!

I'm handy with candy.
I star with a bar.
And I'm known for my butterscotch burp;
I can stare in the eyes
Of a Toffee Surprise
And polish it off with one slurp.
My lick is the longest,
My chomp is the champ
And everyone envies my bite;
But my talents were wasted
Until I had tasted
The wonders of Garbage Delight.

  With a nip and a nibble
  A drip and a dribble
  A dollop, a walloping bite:
  If you want to see grins
  All the way to my shins
  Then give me some Garbage Delight,
    Right now!
  Please pass me the Garbage Delight.

Dennis Lee

15

Look Out!

The witches mumble horrid chants,
You're scolded by five thousand aunts,
    A Martian pulls a fearsome face
    And hurls you into Outer Space,
You're tied in front of whistling trains,
A tomahawk has sliced your brains,
    The tigers snarl, the giants roar,
    You're sat on by a dinosaur.
In vain you're shouting "Help" and "Stop,"
The walls are spinning like a top,
    The earth is melting in the sun
    And all the horror's just begun.
And, oh, the screams, the thumping hearts
That awful night before school starts.

Max Fatchen

The Alien

The alien
Was as round as the moon.
Five legs he had
And his ears played a tune.
His hair was pink
And his knees were green,
He was the funniest thing I'd seen
As he danced in the door
Of his strange spacecraft,
He looked at me—
And laughed and laughed!

Julie Holder

When Ice Cream Grows on Spaghetti Trees

When ice cream grows on spaghetti trees,
And the Sahara Desert grows muddy,
When cats and dogs wear B.V.D.'s
That's the time to study.

Anonymous

I Love to Do My Homework

I love to do my homework,
It makes me feel so good.
I love to do exactly
As my teacher says I should.

I love to do my homework,
I never miss a day.
I even love the men in white
Who are taking me away.

Anonymous

Rattlesnake Meat

A gourmet challenged me to eat
A tiny bit of rattlesnake meat,
Remarking, "Don't look horror-stricken,
You'll find it tastes a lot like chicken."
It did.
Now chicken I cannot eat
Because it tastes like rattlesnake meat.

Ogden Nash

Eels

Eileen Carroll
Had a barrel
Filled with writhing eels
And just for fun
She swallowed one:
Now she knows how it feels.

Spike Milligan

Jellyfish Stew

Jellyfish stew,
I'm loony for you,
I dearly adore you,
oh, truly I do,
you're creepy to see,
revolting to chew,
you slide down inside
with a hullabaloo.

You'rc soggy, you're smelly,
you taste like shampoo,
you bog down my belly
with oodles of goo,
yet I would glue noodles
and prunes to my shoe,
for one oozy spoonful
of jellyfish stew.

Jack Prelutsky

Witch Goes Shopping

Witch rides off
Upon her broom
Finds a space
To park it.
Takes a shiny shopping cart
Into the supermarket.
Smacks her lips and reads
The list of things she needs:

    "Six bats' wings
    Worms in brine
    Ears of toads
    Eight or nine.
    Slugs and bugs
    Snake skins dried
    Buzzard innards
    Pickled, fried."

Witch takes herself
From shelf to shelf
Cackling all the while.
Up and down and up and down and
In and out each aisle.
Out come cans and cartons
Tumbling to the floor.
"This," says Witch, now all a-twitch,
"Is a crazy store.
I CAN'T FIND A SINGLE THING
I AM LOOKING FOR!"

                Lilian Moore

The Porcupine

Rebecca Jane,
a friend of mine,
went out to pat
a porcupine.

She very shortly
came back in,
disgusted with
the porcupin.

"One never, ever
should," said Jane,
"go out and pat
a porcupain!"

N. M. Bodecker

The Porcupine

Any hound a porcupine nudges
Can't be blamed for harbouring grudges.
I know one hound that laughed all winter
At a porcupine that sat on a splinter.

Ogden Nash

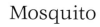

Mosquito

O Mrs. Mosquito, quit biting me, please!
I'm happy my blood type with your type agrees.
　　I'm glad that my flavour
　　Has met with your favour.
　　I'm touched by your care;
　　Yes, I'm touched, everywhere:
On my arms and my legs, on my elbows and knees,
　　Till I cannot tell which
　　Is the itchiest itch
　　Or which itch in the batch
　　Needs the scratchiest scratch.
Your taste for my taste is the reason for these,
So Mrs. Mosquito, quit biting me, please!

Mary Ann Hoberman

Lovely Mosquito

Lovely mosquito, attacking my arm
As quiet and still as a statue,
Stay right where you are! I'll do you no harm—
I simply desire to pat you.

Just puncture my veins and swallow your fill
For, nobody's going to swot you.
Now, lovely mosquito, stay perfectly still—
A SWIPE! and a SPLAT! and I GOT YOU!

Doug MacLeod

Sing Me a Song of Teapots and Trumpets

Sing me a song
of teapots and trumpets:
Trumpots and teapets
and tippets and taps,
trippers and trappers
and jelly bean wrappers
and pigs in pyjamas
with zippers and snaps.

Sing me a song
of sneakers and snoopers:
Snookers and sneapers
and snappers and snacks,
snorkels and snarkles,
a seagull that gargles,
and gargoyles and gryphons
and other knickknacks.

Sing me a song
of parsnips and pickles:
Picsnips and parkles
and pumpkins and pears,
plumbers and mummers
and kettle drum drummers
and plum jam (yum-yum jam)
all over their chairs.

Sing me a song—
but never you mind it!
I've had enough
of this nonsense. Don't cry.
Criers and fliers
and onion ring fryers—
It's more than I want to put up with!
Good-bye!

N. M. Bodecker

Friendly Fredrick Fuddlestone

Friendly Fredrick Fuddlestone
Could fiddle on his funny bone.
When Freddy fiddled
   foolishly fast,
He found his father
   frankly aghast.
Friendly Fredrick Fuddlestone
Kept fiddling on his funny bone.
His furious father
   would flatly forbid it,
Which, of course,
   is why young Freddy did it.

Arnold Lobel

The Ship in the Dock

This ship in the dock was at the end of its trip
The man on deck was the captain of the ship
The name of the captain was Old Ben Brown
He played the ukelele with his trousers down.

Michael Rosen

23

Rhinoceros Stew

If you want to make a rhinoceros stew
all in the world that you have to do
is skin a rhinoceros,
cut it in two
and stew it and stew it and stew it.

When it's stewed so long that you've quite forgot
what it is that's bubbling in the pot
dish it up promptly, serve it hot
and chew it and chew it and chew it

AND CHEW IT AND CHEW IT AND CHEW IT
and chew it and chew it and chew it
and chew it and chew it and chew it

Mildred Luton

Recipe for a Hippopotamus Sandwich

A hippo sandwich is easy to make.
All you do is simply take
One slice of bread,
One slice of cake,
Some mayonnaise,
One onion ring,
One hippopotamus,
One piece of string,
A dash of pepper—
That ought to do it.
And now comes the problem . . .
Biting into it!

Shel Silverstein

24

A Social Mixer

Father said, "Heh, heh! I'll fix her!"—
Threw Mother in the concrete mixer.

She whirled about and called, "Come hither!"
It looked like fun. He jumped in with her.

Then in to join that dizzy dance
Jumped Auntie Bea and Uncle Anse.

In leaped my little sister Lena
And Chuckling Chuck, her pet hyena.

Even Granmaw Fanshaw felt a yearning
To do some high-speed overturning.

All shouted through the motor's whine,
"Aw come on in—the concrete's fine!"

I jumped in too and got all scrambly.
What a crazy mixed-up family!

X. J. Kennedy

Bella Had a New Umbrella

Bella had a new umbrella,
Didn't want to lose it,
So when she walked out in the rain
She didn't ever use it.

Her nose went sniff,
Her shoes went squish,
Her socks grew soggy,
Her glasses got foggy,
Her pockets filled with water
And a little green froggy.

All she could speak was a weak *kachoo*!
But Bella's umbrella
Stayed nice and new.

Eve Merriam

Do Ghouls?

Do ghouls
go out
on a rainy day?

When it
splishes and
sploshes,
do
ghouls
wear
ghoul-oshes?

Lilian Moore

Thunder and Lightning

The thunder crashed
The lightning flashed
And all the world was shaken;
The little pig
Curled up his tail
And ran to save his bacon.

Anonymous

43

Willie Built a Guillotine

Willie built a guillotine,
Tried it out on sister Jean.
Said Mother as she got the mop:
"These messy games have got to stop!"

William E. Engel

The Boy Stood on the Burning Deck

The boy stood on the burning deck,
His feet were full of blisters;
The flames came up and burned his pants,
And now he wears his sister's.

Anonymous

Brother

I had a little brother
And I brought him to my mother
And I said I want another
Little brother for a change.

But she said don't be a bother
So I took him to my father
And I said this little bother
Of a brother's very strange.

But he said one little brother
Is exactly like another
And every little brother
Misbehaves a bit, he said.

So I took the little bother
From my mother and my father
And I put the little bother
Of a brother back to bed.

Mary Ann Hoberman

Mummy Slept Late and Daddy Fixed Breakfast

Daddy fixed the breakfast.
He made us each a waffle.
It looked like gravel pudding.
It tasted something awful.

"Ha, ha," he said, "I'll try again.
This time I'll get it right."
But what *I* got was in between
Bituminous and anthracite.

"A little too well done? Oh well,
I'll have to start all over."
That time what landed on my plate
Looked like a manhole cover.

I tried to cut it with a fork:
The fork gave off a spark.
I tried a knife and twisted it
Into a question mark.

I tried it with a hack-saw.
I tried it with a torch.
It didn't even make a dent.
It didn't even scorch.

The next time Dad gets breakfast
When Mommy's sleeping late,
I think I'll skip the waffles.
I'd sooner eat the plate!

John Ciardi

46

Questions, Quistions & Quoshtions

Daddy how does an elephant feel
When he swallows a piece of steel?
Does he get drunk
And fall on his trunk
Or roll down the road like a wheel?

Daddy what would a pelican do
If he swallowed a bottle of glue?
Would his beak get stuck
Would he run out of luck
And lose his job at thc zoo?

Son tell me tell me true,
If I belted you with a shoe,
Would you fall down dead?
Would you go up to bed?
—Either of those would do.

Spike Milligan

Each Night Father Fills Me with Dread

Each night father fills me with dread
When he sits on the foot of my bed;
   I'd not mind that he speaks
   In gibbers and squcaks,
But for seventeen years he's been dead.

Edward Gorey

Mechanical Menagerie

My Uncle Ike's an engineer.
He has the nutty habit
Of building beasts from wheels and wire.
He's built a robot rabbit

That hides in manholes in the street
And lives on tinfoil lettuce.
His brand new chrome-trimmed crocodile
Keeps trying hard to get us.

He has lightning bugs that come with plugs,
Electric eels that boil,
A bat that flies on batteries,
An oyster that you oil,

A forty-four-seat elephant
With a trunk so you can pack her,
And a parrot that says, "Polly want
A lighted cannon cracker!"

X. J. Kennedy

Night Starvation or The Biter Bit

At night, my Uncle Rufus
(Or so I've heard it said)
Would put his teeth into a glass
Of water by his bed.

At three o'clock one morning
He woke up with a cough,
And as he reached out for his teeth—
They bit his hand right off.

Carey Blyton

Fame Was a Claim of Uncle Ed's

Fame was a claim of Uncle Ed's,
Simply because he had three heads,
Which, if he'd only had a third of,
I think he would never have been heard of.

Ogden Nash

Rules

Do not jump on ancient uncles.
*
Do not yell at average mice.
*
Do not wear a broom to breakfast.
*
Do not ask a snake's advice.
*
Do not bathe in chocolate pudding.
*
Do not talk to bearded bears.
*
Do not smoke cigars on sofas.
*
Do not dance on velvet chairs.
*
Do not take a whale to visit
Russell's mother's cousin's yacht.
*
And whatever else you do do
It is better you
Do not.

Karla Kuskin

My Mother Says I'm Sickening

My mother says I'm sickening,
my mother says I'm crude,
she says this when she sees me
playing Ping-Pong with my food,
she doesn't seem to like it
when I slurp my bowl of stew,
and now she's got a list of things
she says I mustn't do—

DO NOT CATAPULT THE CARROTS!
DO NOT JUGGLE GOBS OF FAT!
DO NOT DROP THE MASHED POTATOES
ON THE GERBIL OR THE CAT!
NEVER PUNCH THE PUMPKIN PUDDING!
NEVER TUNNEL THROUGH THE BREAD!
PUT NO PEAS INTO YOUR POCKET!
PLACE NO NOODLES ON YOUR HEAD!
DO NOT SQUEEZE THE STEAMED ZUCCHINI!
DO NOT MAKE THE MELON OOZE!
NEVER STUFF VANILLA YOGURT
IN YOUR LITTLE SISTER'S SHOES!
DRAW NO FACES IN THE KETCHUP!
MAKE NO LITTLE GRAVY POOLS!

I wish my mother wouldn't make
so many useless rules.

Jack Prelutsky

Learning

I'm learning to say thank you.
And I'm learning to say please.
And I'm learning to use Kleenex,
Not my sweater, when I sneeze.
And I'm learning not to dribble.
And I'm learning not to slurp.
And I'm learning (though it sometimes
    really hurts me)
Not to burp.
And I'm learning to chew softer
When I eat corn on the cob.
And I'm learning that it's much
Much easier to be a slob.

Judith Viorst

Piggy

For breakfast I had ice cream
    With pickles sliced up in it;
For lunch, some greasy pork chops
    Gobbled in a minute;
Dinner? Clams and orange pop,
    And liverwurst, sliced thick—
And now, oops! Oh, pardon me!
    I'm going to be sick!

William Cole

Help

Can anybody tell me, please,
a bit about the thing
with seven legs and furry knees,
four noses and a wing?

Oh what has prickles on its chin,
what's yellow, green and blue,
and what has soft and slimy skin?
Oh tell me, tell me, do.

And tell me, what has polka dots
on every other ear,
what ties its tail in twenty knots,
what weeps a purple tear?

Oh what is growling long and low
and please, has it been fed?
I think I'd really better know . . .
it's sitting on my head.

Jack Prelutsky

Attic Fanatic

As I lie in my bed
Things scratch overhead,
They rustle and scrabble and scurry;
And I've got a feeling
That over the ceiling
Are things that are scaly and furry.

Dad says they're just bats,
I see pythons and rats,
Grizzlies and starved alligators;
Dragony things
With claws, fangs and wings . . .

OH PLEASE CALL THE EXTERMINATOR!!!!!!!

Lois Simmie

Screaming

I hate the sound of screaming—
When horrors pull your hair,
When shutters bang and doorbells clang
But nobody is there.

When yellow eyes are gleaming,
But they are all you see,
I hate the sound of screaming—
Especially when it's me!

Doug MacLeod

First It Bit My Behind

First it bit my behind,
Then it nibbled on my ear.
(I'd rather have my hearing marred
Than toothmarks on my rear.)

Then it took away my sister—
While we all were dining,
It's been about a month now,
All clouds have a silver lining.

Barry Louis Polisar

The Ogglewop

The Ogglewop is tall and wide,
And though he looks quite passive,
He's crammed with boys and girls inside,
—That's why he is so massive!

Colin West

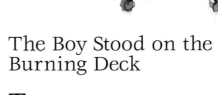

The Dinosore

Poor Dinosore, his body's big,
His tail it weighs a ton,
His head is full of bones and stones,
And when he tries to run

The pounding poundage gets him down.
He gasps and gasps some more.
His aching feet, they have him beat,
That's why he's Dinosore.

Jane Yolen

Gooloo

The Gooloo bird
She has no feet,
She cannot walk
Upon the street.
She cannot build
Herself a nest,
She cannot land
And take a rest.
Through rain and snow
And thundcrous skics,
She weeps forever
As she flies,
And lays her eggs
High over town,
And prays that they
Fall safely down.

Shel Silverstein

The Ombley-Gombley

Once upon a train track
The Ombley-Gombley sat.
Rumble clang,
Jumble jang,
Crumble bang—
And that's the end of that.

Peter Wesley-Smith

Happy Birthday to You

Happy birthday to you,
You live in the zoo,
You smell like a monkey,
And look like one too.

Anonymous

Marguerite

Marguerite, go wash your feet,
The Board of Health's across the street.

Anonymous

There Was a Man Dressed All in Cheese

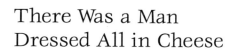

There was a man
Dressed all in cheese.
Certain was he
That the sight would please.
Though his neighbours agreed,
Those clothes looked well on him,
They ran far away
From that certain smell on him.

Arnold Lobel

The Truth About the Abominable Footprint

The Yeti's a Beast
Who lives in the East
    And suffers a lot from B.O.
His hot hairy feet
Stink out the street
    So he cools them off in the snow.

Michael Baldwin

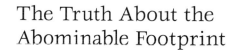

Loose and Limber

Loose and limber,
Beanbag Jim
Seems to have
No bones in him.
At carnivals
And vaudeville shows
He ties himself
In knots and bows.
He's known to all
Throughout the land
As nature's living
Rubber band.

Arnold Lobel

Edward Jones

A skinny man,
   named Edward Jones,
Was nothing but
   a bag of bones.
He filled himself
   with ice cream cones,
And now he's known
   as Cold Bones Jones.

Sol Mandlsohn

Bones

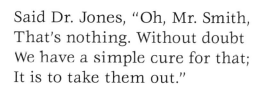

Said Mr. Smith, "I really cannot
Tell you, Dr. Jones,
The most peculiar pain I'm in—
I think it's in my bones."

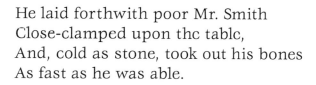

Said Dr. Jones, "Oh, Mr. Smith,
That's nothing. Without doubt
We have a simple cure for that;
It is to take them out."

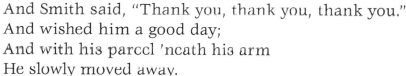

He laid forthwith poor Mr. Smith
Close-clamped upon the table,
And, cold as stone, took out his bones
As fast as he was able.

And Smith said, "Thank you, thank you, thank you."
And wished him a good day;
And with his parcel 'neath his arm
He slowly moved away.

Walter de la Mare

I Thought I'd Take My Rat to School

I thought I'd take my rat to school
    To show my nice new teacher.
       "Aaaeeeiiiiiiieeaa!" she said.
     "Get out, you horrid creature!"

Colin McNaughton

A Mouse in Her Room

A mouse in her room woke Miss Dowd;
She was frightened and screamed very loud,
    Then a happy thought hit her—
    To scare off the critter,
She sat up in bed and meowed.

Anonymous

The Last Cry of the Damp Fly

Bitter batter boop!
I'm swimming in your soup.

Bitter batter bout:
Kindly get me out!

Bitter batter boon:
Not upon your spoon!

Bitter batter bum!
Now I'm in your tum!

Dennis Lee

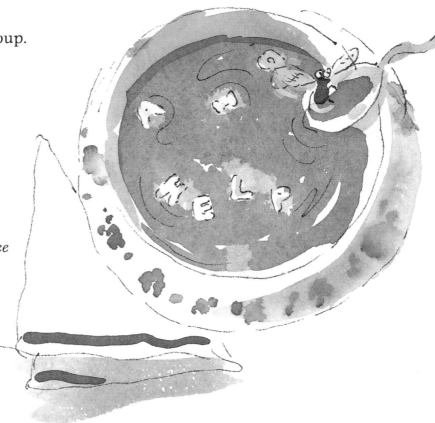

Goodnight, Sleep Tight

Goodnight, sleep tight.
Don't let the bedbugs bite.
If they do, get your shoe
And hit them till they're black and blue.

Anonymous

63

Never Take a Pig to Lunch

Never take a pig to lunch.
Don't invite him home for brunch.
Cancel chances to be fed
Till you're certain he's well-bred.

Quiz him! Can he use a spoon?
Does his sipping sing a tune?
Will he slurp and burp and snuff
Till his gurgling makes you gruff?

Would he wrap a napkin 'round
Where the dribbled gravy's found?
Tidbits nibble? Doughnuts dunk?
Spill his milk before it's drunk?

Root and snoot through soup du jour?
Can your appetite endure?
If his manners make you moan,
Better let him lunch alone.

Susan Alton Schmeltz

Sneaky Bill

I'm Sneaky Bill, I'm terrible mean and vicious,
I steal all the cashews
    from the mixed-nuts dishes;
I eat all the icing but I won't touch the cake,
And what you won't give me,
    I'll go ahead and take.

I gobble up the cherries from everyone's drinks,
And whenever there are sausages
    I grab a dozen links;
I take both drumsticks if
    there's turkey or chicken,
And the biggest strawberries
    are what I'm pickin';

I make sure I get the finest chop on the plate,
And I'll eat the portions of anyone who's late!

I'm always on the spot before the dinner bell—
I guess I'm pretty awful,
                        but
                          I
                            do
                              eat
                                well!

William Cole

Stealing Eggs

Stealing eggs, Fritz ran afoul
Of an angry great horned owl.
Now she has him—what a catch!—
Seeing if his head will hatch.

X. J. Kennedy

The Angry Hens from Never-when

The angry hens from Never-when
had a fight and lost their legs.
Now it's hot
where they squat
and they're laying soft-boiled eggs.

Michael Rosen

66

Our Canary

Our canary is dusty and cold and mad,
She sits around in a rage
Since we sucked her up in the vacuum hose
While cleaning out her cage.
Her feathers stayed behind in the bag
When we blew her out the end . . .

We're sending her off to Florida
Till her feathers grow in again.

Lois Simmie

When You Stand
on the Tip of Your Nose

When you stand on the tip of your nose,
keeping perfectly still,
while the birds build their nests twixt
   your toes,
as they certainly will,
speak kind and encouraging words,
don't wiggle however it goes,
as you might inconvenience the birds
or scramble their eggs with your toes.

N. M. Bodecker

Habits of the Hippopotamus

The hippopotamus is strong
  And huge of head and broad of bustle;
The limbs on which he rolls along
  Are big with hippopotomuscle.

He does not greatly care for sweets
  Like ice cream, apple pie, or custard,
But takes to flavour what he eats
  A little hippopotomustard.

The hippopotamus is true
  To all his principles, and just;
He always tries his best to do
  The things one hippopotomust.

He never rides in trucks or trams,
  In taxicabs or omnibuses,
And so keeps out of traffic jams
  And other hippopotomusses.

Arthur Guiterman

Mules

On mules we find two legs behind,
  And two we find before,
We stand behind before we find
  What the two behind be for.
When we're behind the two behind
  We find what these be for,
So stand before the two behind,
  Behind the two before.

Anonymous

68

Sea Horse and Sawhorse

A sea horse saw a sawhorse
On a seesaw meant for two.
"See here, sawhorse," said sea horse,
"May I seesaw with you?"

"I'll see, sea horse," said sawhorse.
"Right now I'm having fun
Seeing if I'll be seasick
On a seesaw meant for one."

X. J. Kennedy

Eletelephony

Once there was an elephant,
Who tried to use the telephant—
No! no! I mean an elephone
Who tried to use the telephone—
(Dear me! I am not certain quite
That even now I've got it right.)

Howe'er it was, he got his trunk
Entangled in the telephunk;
The more he tried to get it free,
The louder buzzed the telephee—
(I fear I'd better drop the song
Of elephop and telephong!)

Laura E. Richards

My Dog

My dog is such a gentle soul,
Although he's big it's true.
He brings the paper in his mouth.
He brings the postman too.

Max Fatchen

Raising Frogs for Profit

Raising frogs for profit
Is a very sorry joke.
How can you make money
When so many of them croak?

Anonymous

Three Little Monkeys

I know something I won't tell—
Three little monkeys in a peanut shell!
One can sing and one can dance,
And one can make a pair of pants.

Anonymous

The Alligator

The alligator chased his tail
Which hit him on the snout;
He nibbled, gobbled, swallowed it,
And turned right inside-out.

Mary MacDonald

The Giggles

A giggler gets the giggles
  At every little thing—
A puppy dog that sneezes,
  A cow that tries to sing.

She giggles at an elephant,
  She giggles at a toad.
She giggles if a baby duck
  Waddles down a road.

She giggles if the teacher asks
  If two and two are four.
At lunch she giggles if she spills
  Potatoes on the floor.

When Mother sat on Daddy's hat
  She giggled till she cried.
I think she ate a feather that
  Is tickling her inside!

Martin Gardner

72

Ode to a Sneeze

I sneezed a sneeze into the air.
It fell to earth I know not where,
But hard and froze were the looks of those
In whose vicinity I snoze.

George Wallace

Chimney Squirrels

Chimney squirrels
cough a lot,
topple off
the roof a lot,

So why do you
suppose they choose
to roast and sneeze
among the flues?

The only answer
seems to be
(it only just
occurred to me),

They *had* to take
the chimney nook,
for every other
tree was took!

John Goldthwaite

Whose Boo Is Whose?

Two ghosts I know once traded heads
And shrieked and shook their sheets to shreds—
"You're me!" yelled one, "and me, I'm you!
Now who can boo the loudest boo?"

"Me!" cried the other, and for proof
He booed a boo that scared the ròof
Right off our house. Our TV set
Jumped higher than a jumbo jet.

The first ghost snickered. "Why, you creep,
Call that a boo? that feeble beep?
Hear *this!*"—and sucking in a blast
Of wind, he puffed his sheet so vast

And booed so hard, a passing goose
Lost all its down. The moon shook loose
And fell and smashed to smithereens—
Stars scattered like spilled jellybeans.

"How's that for booing, boy? I win,"
Said one. The other scratched a chin
Where only bone was—"Win or lose?
How can we tell whose boo is whose?"

X. J. Kennedy

Punch and Judy

Punch and Judy
   Fought for a pie;
Punch gave Judy
   A knock in the eye.
Says Punch to Judy,
   Will you have any more?
Says Judy to Punch,
   My eye is too sore.

Anonymous

Adolphus

Adolphus is despicable—
Before the day begins,
To prove that I am kickable,
He kicks me in the shins.

Colin West

The Bluffalo

Oh, do not tease the Bluffalo
With quick-step or with shuffalo
When you are in a scuffalo
In Bluffalo's backyard.

For it has quite enoughalo
Of people playing toughalo
And when it gives a cuffalo
It gives it very hard.

But if by chance a scuffalo
Occurs twixt you and Bluffalo,
Pray tempt it with a truffalo
And catch it off its guard.

And while it eats that stuffalo
You can escape the Bluffalo
And with a huff and puffalo
Depart from its backyard.

Jane Yolen

Is It Possicle?

There once was a sweet little Mousicle
  (An especially good kind of mouse),
Who lived with his friend in a housicle
  (An especially good kind of house).
   He rode a bicycle,
   She rode a tricycle,
Exactly the size for the mice.
On Sunday they feasted on strawberry icicle.
Strawberry icicle's awfully nicicle.
  (And nicicle's nicer than nice.)

Marion Edey

A Big Bare Bear

A big bare bear
   bought a bear balloon,
For a big bear trip
   to the bare, bare moon.
A hairy bear
   saw the bare bear fly
On his big bear trip
   in the bare, bare sky.
The hairy bear
   took a jet up high
To catch the bear
   in the big bare sky.
The hairy bear
   flew his jet right by
The bear balloon
   in the big bare sky.
He popped the balloon
   with his hairy thumb,
And the bare bear fell
   on his big bum bum.

Robert Heidbreder

Bursting

We've laughed until my cheeks are tight.
We've laughed until my stomach's sore.
If we could only stop we might
Remember what we're laughing for.

Dorothy Aldis

AUTHOR INDEX

TITLE INDEX

Acknowledgements

The editors and publishers wish to thank the following for giving permission to include in this anthology material which is their copyright. If we have inadvertently omitted to acknowledge anyone we should be most grateful if this could be brought to our attention for correction at the first opportunity.

Addison-Wesley Publishing Company, Inc., for "Oodles of Noodles" from *Oodles of Noodles* by Lucia and James L. Hymes, Jr. Copyright © 1964 by Lucia and James L. Hymes, Jr. Reprinted by permission of the publisher.

Michael Baldwin and Partners for "The Truth About the Abominable Footprint" by Michael Baldwin.

Carey Blyton for "Night Starvation or The Biter Bit." Reprinted by permission of Carey Blyton, composer/author.

Curtis Brown, Ltd., for "The Dinosore" and "The Bluffalo" by Jane Yolen. Copyright © 1980 by Jane Yolen. "Rattlesnake Meat" excerpted from "Splinters from the Festive Board" by Ogden Nash. Copyright © 1968 by Ogden Nash. "Fame was a Claim of Uncle Ed's" from *The Primrose Path* by Ogden Nash. Copyright 1935 by Ogden Nash. "Sea Horse and Sawhorse," "A Social Mixer," and "Mechanical Menagerie" by X. J. Kennedy. Copyright © 1975 by X. J. Kennedy. "Whose Boo Is Whose?" by X. J. Kennedy. Copyright © 1979 by X. J. Kennedy. All selections reprinted by permission of Curtis Brown, Ltd.

Judith H. Ciardi for "Some Cook!" from *The Man Who Sang the Sillies* (Lippincott, 1961) by John Ciardi. Permission granted by Judith H. Ciardi, sole beneficiary of The Estate of John Ciardi.

William Cole for "Banananananananana," "News Story," "Piggy," and "Sneaky Bill." Copyright © 1977 by William Cole.

Collins/Angus & Robertson Publishers for "The Dodo" and "The Ombley-Gombley" from *The Ombley-Gombley* by Peter Wesley-Smith. Copyright © 1969 by Peter Wesley-Smith & David Fielding. Reprinted by permission of Collins/Angus & Robertson Publishers.

Andre Deutsch Ltd., for "The Parent" and "The Porcupine" from *I Wouldn't Have Missed It* by Ogden Nash. Copyright 1933, 1944 by Ogden Nash. First appeared in *The Saturday Evening Post*. Reprinted by permission of Andre Deutsch Ltd.

Douglas & McIntyre Ltd. for "Attic Fanatic," "Neet People," and "Our Canary" from *Auntie's Knitting a Baby* by Lois Simmie. Copyright © 1984 by Lois Simmie. Reprinted by permission of Douglas & McIntyre Ltd.

Farrar, Straus & Giroux, Inc., for "Anteater" and "Laughing Time" from *Laughing Time* by William Jay Smith. Copyright © 1955, 1957, 1980, 1990 by William Jay Smith. Reprinted by permission of Farrar, Straus & Giroux, Inc.

Martin Gardner for "The Giggles" from *Never Make Fun of a Turtle, My Son* by Martin Gardner.

John Goldthwaite for "Chimney Squirrels" from *Eggs Amen!* by John Goldthwaite. Copyright © 1973 by John Goldthwaite.

HarperCollins Publishers for "About the Teeth of Sharks," "How to Tell a Tiger," and "Mummy Slept Late and Daddy Fixed Breakfast" from *You Read to Me, I'll Read to You* (Lippincott) by John Ciardi, illustrated by Edward Gorey. Copyright © 1962 by John Ciardi. "A Bug Sat in a Silver Flower," "Hughbert and the Glue," "Me," and "Rules" from *Dogs & Dragons, Trees & Dreams* by Karla Kuskin. "A Bug Sat in a Silver Flower" originally appeared in *Near the Window Tree* by Karla Kuskin. Copyright © 1975 by Karla Kuskin. "Jake, the Twin of John Lothario" from *Silly Songs and Sad* (T. Y. Crowell) by Ellen Raskin. Copyright © 1967 by Ellen Raskin. All selections reprinted by permission of HarperCollins Publishers.

Heinemann Young Books for "Be Glad Your Nose Is on Your Face," "Forty Performing Bananas," "Jellyfish Stew," and "My Mother Says I'm Sickening" from *The New Kid on the Block* by Jack Prelutsky. Copyright © 1984 by Jack Prelutsky.

Houghton Mifflin Company for "At the Beach" from *Doodle Soup* by John Ciardi. Copyright © 1985 by Myra J. Ciardi. Reprinted by permission of Houghton Mifflin Company.

Bobbi Katz for "Morning" from *Upside Down and Inside Out: Poems for All Your Pockets*. Copyright © 1976 by Bobbi Katz. Used with permission of the author who controls all rights.

Little, Brown & Company for "Eletelephony" from *Tirra Lirra: Rhymes Old and New* by Laura E. Richards. Copyright © renewed 1960 by Hamilton Richards. Reprinted by permission of Little, Brown & Company.

Mildred Luton for "Rhinoceros Stew." Reprinted by permission of the author, Mildred Luton.

Gina Maccoby Literary Agency for "Brother" from *Yellow Butter Purple Jelly Red Jam Black Bread* by Mary Ann Hoberman. Copyright © 1959, renewed 1987 by Mary Ann Hoberman. "Mosquito" from *Bugs* by Mary Ann Hoberman. Copyright © 1976 by Mary Ann Hoberman. "Nuts to You and Nuts to Me" by Mary Ann Hoberman. Copyright © 1974 by Mary Ann Hoberman. All selections reprinted by permission of Gina Maccoby Literary Agency.

Macmillan Publishing Company for "When You Stand on the Tip of Your Nose" and "Sing Me a Song of Teapots and Trumpets," reprinted with permission of Margaret K. McElderry Books, an imprint of Macmillan Publishing Company, from *Hurry, Hurry, Mary Dear! And Other Nonsense Poems* by N. M. Bodecker. Copyright © 1976 by N. M. Bodecker. "The Porcupine" reprinted with permission of Margaret K. McElderry Books, an imprint of Macmillan Publishing Company, from *Let's Marry Said the Cherry and Other Nonsense Poems* by N. M. Bodecker. Copyright © 1974 by N. M. Bodecker. "Stealing Eggs" reprinted with permission of Margaret K. McElderry Books, an imprint of Macmillan Publishing Company, from *Brats* by X. J. Kennedy. Copyright © 1986 by X. J. Kennedy. "Is It Possible?" reprinted with permission of Charles Scribner's Sons, an imprint of Macmil-

Some bestselling Red Fox picture books

THE BIG ALFIE AND ANNIE ROSE STORYBOOK
by Shirley Hughes
OLD BEAR
by Jane Hissey
OI! GET OFF OUR TRAIN
by John Burningham
DON'T DO THAT!
by Tony Ross
NOT NOW, BERNARD
by David McKee
ALL JOIN IN
by Quentin Blake
THE WHALES' SONG
by Gary Blythe and Dyan Sheldon
JESUS' CHRISTMAS PARTY
by Nicholas Allan
THE PATCHWORK CAT
by Nicola Bayley and William Mayne
MATILDA
by Hilaire Belloc and Posy Simmonds
WILLY AND HUGH
by Anthony Browne
THE WINTER HEDGEHOG
by Ann and Reg Cartwright
A DARK, DARK TALE
by Ruth Brown
HARRY, THE DIRTY DOG
by Gene Zion and Margaret Bloy Graham
DR XARGLE'S BOOK OF EARTHLETS
by Jeanne Willis and Tony Ross
WHERE'S THE BABY?
by Pat Hutchins